**Genre** Fiction

MW00490007

Matt's Journey

by Clara Strongfoot

illustrated by Margeaux Lucas

Chapter 1
Gloomy Day

Matt looked out the window at another rainy day. "Why does it always have to rain on Saturdays?" Matt thought. "Why couldn't it be a sunny day just once? *Why?*"

The rain splashed against the window, blurring Matt's view. Matt stared harder.

"I see shapes moving outside," he thought. "Hmmm, what can they be?" Then Matt noticed that the rain sounded like a drumbeat as it tapped against the window.

The blurry shapes began to move. "Some of them look like people," Matt thought. "Others look like animals. But I can't see their faces clearly through the wet glass."

Matt kept gazing at the moving shapes. Then he smiled and let his imagination take over.

STOP AND CHECK

What does Matt think he sees outside?

Chapter 2
Rainforest Dance

A jungle set deep in a rainforest spread before Matt's eyes. "I can see people dancing," he thought. "They're surrounded by jungle plants and animals."

Matt couldn't tell if the dancers were men or women. They were wearing animal masks. "Those are cool masks! I wish I had one," thought Matt.

The rain continued its steady beat. Matt felt the drumbeat in his body. He swayed from side to side.

Then Matt heard the masked people calling to him. "Come and join us!" they shouted. "Dance with us!"

Matt wanted to join the dancers. He went into the jungle. Soon he was dancing and wearing a mask.

The drumbeat got stronger and stronger. The dancing got faster and faster. Matt was trying his best to keep up. Then he heard a knocking sound. It was a clap of thunder.

"Matt!" Mom's voice broke through his daydream. She was knocking on his door. She opened it and peeked inside.

"Is everything all right?" she asked. Matt nodded, still looking out the window. The masked people were gone now. The rain had stopped, and the sun was out.

"Come into the kitchen," Mom said. "I have your lunch ready."

STOP AND CHECK

What does Matt imagine doing in the jungle?

Chapter 3
Desert Ride

Matt sat down to eat lunch. Dazzling sunlight shone through the window. The heat of the sun warmed him.

"It feels hot," he thought, "almost as hot as a desert!" Matt looked out and saw a man walking his dog. "That dog is pretty big," he said. "But maybe it's not a dog after all. Maybe it's really a camel!"

Matt let his imagination create a
new scene. The walls of his house
disappeared. The sidewalks and lawns
of his neighborhood faded. He was
surrounded by sandy dunes, standing
next to a man and a camel.

Matt patted the camel. "Hi there,
big fellow," he said.

The camel winked at Matt. "Climb
on," the camel seemed to say.

The camel kneeled, and Matt
climbed on its back. The next thing
he knew, he was galloping across
the desert.

"Wow! This is more fun than
go-carts!" thought Matt.

"Matt?" His mom's voice startled him. "Aren't you hungry, dear?"

Matt blinked a few times. The camel was gone. So were the sandy dunes.

STOP AND CHECK

What kind of animal does the dog become in Matt's mind?

Chapter 4

A Big Appetite

Matt looked at his sandwich.
Suddenly, his mouth was a dry desert
full of sand.

"Boy, am I thirsty!" said Matt. He
got up to get a drink of water, then
sat back down and gobbled up his
lunch. "Boy, am I hungry!" he said.

Matt finished his lunch quickly. A few seconds later, he asked Mom for some more fruit.

"What did you do all morning that made you so hungry?" Mom asked.

"Well, first I danced in the rainforest. Then I rode a camel through the desert," Matt replied.

"Well, then, I guess you need to feed your imagination," Mom said.

Matt grinned and nodded. So far, it had been an exciting Saturday.

STOP AND CHECK

Why is Matt so hungry?

Respond to Reading

Summarize

Use important details to summarize *Matt's Journey*.

Character	Clue	Point of View

Text Evidence

1. How do you know *Matt's Journey* is fiction? Genre

2. How does Matt feel about the rain at first? Point of View

3. What is the metaphor on page 13? Metaphors

4. Write about Matt's point of view and his mother's point of view. Write About Reading

Compare Texts

Now read some poems about where your imagination can take you.

Autumn Leaves

Fall leaves fly and float,
Tiny boats sailing on air.
Gusts of wind send them twirling,
Skipping from here to there.

Dancing and prancing
All along the ground,
Under my boots, they
Make a crunching sound.

The Orchestra

The orchestra, oh, the orchestra!
We're off to see the orchestra.
Instruments large and small
   Take me places by ear.

The orchestra, oh, the orchestra!
Giant kettle drums roar.
Thunder and lightning
   Rumble in the sky.

The orchestra, oh, the orchestra!
Takes my breath away.
Flutes fly me to a meadow
    Of flowers and sunshine.

The orchestra, oh, the orchestra!
Loud and strong, soft and gentle.
So many skilled hands
    Take me places by ear.

Make Connections
Where did Matt go? Essential Question
How can sounds help you imagine
other places? Text to Text

Focus on
Literary Elements

Dialogue Dialogue is the words characters speak in a story. Dialogue can help you understand a character's thoughts and feelings.

What to Look for As you read, look for quotation marks. They look like this: " ". They show what characters say. Look at this example.

"Is everything all right?" she asked.

Your Turn

Write a story that has characters speaking to each other. Use quotation marks around the words each character says.